The Ultimate Tea Guide

A Detailed List of 60+ Tea Varieties, including Health Benefits & Steeping Recommendations

by Kathleen Rao

Table of Contents

Introduction 1

Chapter 1 – General Health Benefits of Tea 7

Chapter 2 – Green Tea (Varieties, Health Benefits, Steeping) 13

Chapter 3 – Black Tea (Varieties, Health Benefits, Steeping) 23

Chapter 4 – White Tea (Varieties, Health Benefits, Steeping) 31

Chapter 5 – Oolong Tea (Varieties, Health Benefits, Steeping) 37

Chapter 6 – Rooibos Tea (Varieties, Health Benefits, Steeping) 43

Chapter 7 – Herbal Tea (Varieties, Health Benefits, Steeping) 47

Conclusion 53

Introduction

The media is abuzz with information aimed at helping people lead a healthier and happier life. Everybody wants to live long while feeling good and looking amazing. This universal desire has led to the introduction of countless beauty products, many of which are expensive yet ineffective. But in the midst of these hullabaloos, there is something that actually can help you achieve a longer, healthier, and happier life – and it's all natural too.

Tea has been with us for years, and almost every culture will tell you that they have a way of preparing and enjoying it, even if some do not understand or consider the amazing health benefits associated with the cup they take. Tea is available on the market today and you can get it in countless different flavors, types, and combinations. Some types of teas are more commonly known than others.

Research has revealed that drinking different types of tea has a way of altering cellular count and health in the body thus improving your health while at the same time slowing down the natural process of aging. Tea has also been found to be a good stimulant and it does help to calm and revitalize the nervous system. In general, some of the benefits associated with different types of teas include the following:

- Promoting health and enhancing quality of life
- Boosting immunity and reducing chances of contracting a host of diseases
- Relieving stress, anxiety and calming the nervous system
- Relieving the body from symptoms associated with different health complications
- Detoxification of the body to rid it of impurities
- Preventing a range of chronic diseases

There are many other benefits associated with drinking tea as will be discussed in the first chapter. Everyone should consider including different types of teas in their day-to-day life so as to enjoy the amazing benefits provided by this natural product. Remember, different types of teas have different health benefits and therefore you should seek to familiarize yourself with a range of teas in order to seek out and appreciate the type that will next fill your cup and grace your tongue.

But all of the above is probably just preaching to the choir, because you're here reading this, which means you already know how beneficial tea can be. Now you just need a thorough list of the various options including their specific benefits and characteristics so you can explore the gamut of tea delight available. Let's get started!

© Copyright 2014 by LCPublifish LLC - All rights reserved.

This document is geared towards providing reliable information in regards to the topic and issue covered. The publication is sold with the idea that the publisher is not required to render accounting, officially permitted, or otherwise, qualified services. If advice is necessary, legal or professional, a practiced individual in the profession should be ordered.

- From a Declaration of Principles which was accepted and approved equally by a Committee of the American Bar Association and a Committee of Publishers and Associations.

In no way is it legal to reproduce, duplicate, or transmit any part of this document in either electronic means or in printed format. Recording of this publication is strictly prohibited and any storage of this document is not allowed unless with written permission from the publisher. All rights reserved.

The information provided herein is stated to be truthful and consistent, in that any liability, in terms of inattention or otherwise, by any usage or abuse of any policies, processes, or directions contained within is solely and completely the responsibility of the recipient reader. Under no circumstances will any legal responsibility or blame be held against the publisher for any reparation, damages, or monetary loss due to the information herein, either directly or indirectly.

Respective authors own all copyrights not held by the publisher.

The information herein is offered for informational purposes solely, and is universal as so. The presentation of the information is without contract or any type of guarantee assurance.

The trademarks that are used are without any consent, and the publication of the trademark is without permission or backing by the trademark owner. All trademarks and brands within this book are for clarifying purposes only and are the owned by the owners themselves, not affiliated with this document.

Chapter 1 – General Health Benefits of Tea

Before discussing the different types of teas and their specific benefits, it's important to have an in-depth look at the general benefits of tea as a whole. While each type of tea has its unique benefits, there are some advantages that are generally associated with tea and you should appreciate these regardless of what variety you select.

Tea Affects Your Emotions and Physical Health

A warm or hot cup of tea is always refreshing, relaxing, and comforting especially after a long stressful day. This simply means that tea consumption has an impact on your emotional health which in turn affects or correlates with your physical health. Tea has been found universally suitable for calming nerves and thus has been used for years as a stress reliever. Research has shown that stress is normally caused by a kind of imbalance which takes place in the stress hormones, and that drinking a cup of hot or warm tea helps bring a balance to these hormones thus helping the body to relax. It is therefore understandable that tea has the power to help in the prevention of some serious stress-related diseases including heart disease and adrenal imbalance. According to research, people who drink tea regularly during the day have a lower rate of stress and stress-related diseases. Also, research has shown tea to greatly improve psychological health and prevent or relieve symptoms of depression.

Tea Helps in Weight Loss and Weight Management

Obesity has over the years become a major concern throughout the world especially in the United States. It is important to note that while there are many methods and tips that have been floated as "key" in fighting obesity and managing weight, tea is an essential tool that you cannot ignore. Tea has also been found to be helpful in dealing with cases of diabetes as it helps bring stability in blood sugar levels in the body. In fact, drinking oolong tea has been identified as one of the best methods to control the effects of blood sugar associated with carbohydrates in people with type-2 diabetes.

As for weight loss and weight management, green tea has been found to be useful because of the presence of phyto-chemicals which contain a powerful antioxidant substance known as catechins. This substance, according to research, can help improve the body's ability to lose belly fat if consumed between exercises. It is also beneficial for people who might not be very active since it helps reduce the level of triglyceride. To get these benefits, it's important to drink green tea on a daily basis.

Green tea has also been found to be good for fat metabolism in the liver, where it can also help prevent the accumulation of fatty deposits. Since it works as a detoxifier, green tea will definitely help you enjoy a youthful feel and look.

Tea Can Support Immunity

Green tea is helpful in boosting immunity against cold and flu symptoms. Green tea has some properties that can help you recover from colds and flu faster, and research has shown that people who frequently drink pure green tea enjoy higher immunity against related symptoms. You can easily boost your immunity by drinking tea since it contains L-theanine that activates T-cells, which are part of your immune system and are good at fighting infections. A high concentration of this substance can be obtained from shade-grown green teas. There are also other substances found in tea including catechins or polyphenols which are very good and offer great antiviral and anti-inflammatory effects.

Tea Reduces the Risks of Chronic Diseases

Although tea is not a standalone solution against chronic diseases such as cancer, research has shown that green tea for example is very helpful in preventing cells from turning cancerous. In addition, research has shown that drinking black and green tea helps prevent cases of prostate cancer, cancer of the blood, mouth, ovaries, breast, colon and gastric as well. Recent research has also pointed to the benefits of black tea in reducing the risks of developing Parkinson's disease, while green tea is helpful in slowing down its progression.

The Six Categories of Tea

There are six primary categories of teas on the market today: green, white, black, oolong, roobois, and herbal. The different types of teas offer different levels of benefits and can be used to boost health and promote longevity, prevent and treat diseases, boost physical and emotional health, and sharpen the alertness of mind.

As aforementioned, the different types of teas are highly beneficial but the level of benefits you can get from these teas is largely determined by the level of polyphenols they contain. This is true despite the fact that all these teas are harvested from the same plant. However, each type of tea is extracted from different parts of the tea plant and the process of preparation is different, and thus the distinction. For example, black tea is lower in catechins as compared to green tea. On the other hand, green tea does not have the flavonoids known as aflavins which are present in black tea. It is therefore important to consume different types of teas in order to benefit from all the different substances offered by each.

Chapter 2 – Green Tea (Varieties, Health Benefits, Steeping)

Green Tea is arguably the common most tea in many homes today. Due to the growing understanding of the health benefits associated with tea, green tea has grown in popularity. There are different types of green tea on the market but before we delve into that, it's important to note that this tea is harvested from the tea plant or Camellia Sinensis. The method used to process green tea is different from that used to process other types of teas. Generally, green tea involves the harvesting of tea leaves which are then pan fried or steamed soon after harvesting. This process helps prevent oxidation and thus retains the original green color while keeping the leaves pliable and soft. It should be noted that green tea does have some caffeine.

Different Types of Green Tea

There are many different types of green teas, resulting from the different method of harvesting, country of origin, and weather patterns in the area of cultivation. The different types of green teas are likely to have different flavors. Although green teas are harvested from the same plant, their appearance varies greatly and the results you get when brewing will also vary from one type to the other. However, there is a general consensus as far as the benefits associated with these teas are concerned. Below are some of the most common types of green teas:

List of Green Teas (17 Varieties)

Kai Hua Long Ding: - This green tea is made from very short and very thick leaves. It is grown in the Zhejian Province of China. Its flavor is flowery, sweet, refreshing, and a bit nutty.

Green Snail Spring: - This tea, also known as Pi Lo Chun, is very rare because its cultivation is done in a unique way. First, it is grown among peach, apricot, and plum trees, thus giving it the aroma of the surrounding fruit buds. The tea leaves have a snail-like appearance during rolling. Generally, the Pi Lo Chun green tea is grown in Chinese province of Zhejian. It's flavor is fresh, sweet, and fruity.

Tian Mu Qing Ding: - This is a unique Chinese tea grown in Zhejian province's mountainous regions of Tian Mu, hence its name. It has delicate and fine leaves, produces a light, sweet taste, and thus it should never be over-steeped due to its imperviousness.

Gunpowder: - This green tea is very popular not only in China but also in the United States. Once processed, it has an appearance of tiny pellets which will loosen up during the brewing process. It is normally grown in China's Zhejian

Province, although other regions are quickly embracing its cultivation.

Long Jing or Dragonwell green tea: - This is among the famous green teas in China and the most popular in the United States. It's said that President Richard Nixon drank this tea on his trip to China. It is grown in the Chinese tea-growing region of Zhejian Province and its leaves are flat and jade-colored upon processing. It's known for its sweet orchid-like smell.

Xin Yang Mao Jian: - This green tea has very fine and delicate leaves. It is grown in the Chinese province of Henan. In many places, it's commonly referred to as "green tip". It's flavor is considered sweet, refreshing, and a bit floral.

Snowy Mountain Jian: - This green tea has very long leaves. It is cultivated in high attitudes within the Chinese province of Yunnan. The processing for this green tea is generally different from that of other green teas which gives it a full body flavor that is almost similar to black teas. It is strong and pungent, yet surprisingly smooth, sweet, and floral still.

Hou Kui: - This tea also goes by the popular name "monkey tea". It is grown among orchid trees and thus has an orchid flavor. It is normally grown in the Chinese province of

Anhui. Monkey tea's flavor can be best described as complex, yet sweet and floral.

Hyson Lucky Dragon: - This is a quality hyson green tea, from the Anhui Province of China, whose leaves come in a greenish-yellowish appearance. It has a more full-body flavor as compared to other green teas.

Ceylon green tea: - This tea, produced in Sri Lanka, is known to have a stronger and more aromatic flavor than other green teas, and is very rich in antioxidants. It's said that it takes an acquired taste to drink Ceylon green tea as compared to traditional Japanese and Chinese green teas, because the flavor is less grassy yet bolder.

Sencha: - This Japanese green tea is highly popular. It comes in different types and qualities but is generally processed by exposing the tea leaves to direct sunlight. The flavor of this tea is determined primarily by the season in which its harvested. One of the popular types of Sencha is known as "new tea" or Shincha and is known to be the most delicious of all. It is harvested during the early quarter of the year and mostly prepared through infusion. Sencha comes in a greenish-golden color. You can modify the flavor of Sencha depending on the temperature of water in which it steeps. If you're looking for a mellow flavor, use water that's not as hot; but if you want it to taste more astringent, then use slightly hotter water. Its flavor is said to be rich, refreshing, and hearty similar to "steamed vegetables."

Matcha: - This green tea is grown in the shade, and is often purchased in a powdered form. It is a common tea in the Japanese tea ceremony and is manufactured in the Japanese region of Uji. Matcha green tea is prepared early before harvesting and the tea bushes are covered to protect them from direct sunlight, causes the leaves to change into dark-green, while enhancing the production of amino acids especially L-theanine. After several weeks of covering, the finest buds are picked. The harvested leaves are then separated from each other to set aside those that are rolled out prior to the drying process. The rolled-out leaves are commonly known as gyokuro or jade dew tea, a type of green tea which will be discussed below. The leaves that are laid out will be left to dry, crumbled and then are de-stemmed, de-veined and stone grounded to come up with Matcha. It's best described as tasting smooth, silky, and vegetable-flavored.

Kukicha: - Kukicha green tea comes from white stalks that are produced by harvesting 3 leaves and a bud. This Japanese tea tastes like chestnut and the flavor is caused by the twigs found in the tea. It is a very unusual tea that can even be described as tasting a bit like sesame seeds.

Genmaicha Green Tea: - This Japanese green tea is also referred to as "Popcorn tea". It falls under sencha tea but is first of all pan fried before being blended with toasted hulled rice. During the toasting, the hulled rice will "pop' and thus the name "popcorn tea". Its flavor is smooth, nutty, and plant-like.

Gyokuro tea: - Gyokuro is produced from flat and pointed tea leaves and offers smooth flavor with a light aroma. This Japanese tea is considered to be among the best green teas, tasting both sweet and bright. A few weeks before harvesting, the leaves are shielded from direct sunlight by moving them to the shade.

Houjicha tea: - Houjicha green tea is made from roasted Japanese tea leaves and this gives it a brown color. It has low caffeine levels due to the roasting process and its taste is somewhat nutty.

Bancha: - This Japanese green tea is normally harvested during the late weeks of the harvesting season. Bancha green tea leaves are normally hard and large and the stalks and stems are included during the picking process. Bancha doesn't have a strong flavor compared to other green teas.

Green Tea Steeping Recommendations

To get the best results, you'll need to be careful to steep your green tea correctly. This should be done by heating your water to 185 degrees F (80 °C), or boil and then let cool for about 3 minutes. Green tea should be steeped for 2-3 minutes before separating the tea from the leaves. Drink when the temperature becomes comfortable for you.

Health Benefits of Green Tea

Due to the presence of antioxidants and other nutrients, green tea is very healthy and incredibly helpful to the body. Your cup of green tea will definitely be loaded with different polyphenols including Epigallocatechin Gallate (EGCG), catechins and flavonoids, which work as influential antioxidants. Some of the benefits associated with green tea include:

- Green tea helps to protect cells and molecules from damage and reduce the development of free radicals. The free radicals are responsible for numerous diseases and also play a role in the aging process.

- Green tea is rich in caffeine which is a powerful stimulant. It will help keep your mind alert. Caffeine also blocks Adenosine, an inhibitory neurotransmitter thus boosting the concentration of neurotransmitters such as norepinephrine and dopamine and firing of neurons thus improving the performance of your brain.

- The presence of amino acid L-theanine also helps as an anti-anxiety effect by crossing the blood-brain barrier. L-theanine also increases the production of alpha waves and dopamine in the brain improving the functionality of the brain.

- Green teas enhance fat burning in the body and thus they are ideal for helping improve physical performance. The tea increases the rate of metabolism in the body thus aiding in fat burning.

- Green tea also has antioxidants that aid in lowering different types of cancer. By checking the oxidative damage on the cells, the antioxidants offer protection thus enhancing the health of the cells.

- Green tea offers protection to the brain especially in old age thus lowering the detrimental risks of Parkinson's disease and Alzheimer.

- Green tea also has properties that are helpful in reducing the risk of heart diseases since they help lower triglycerides, LDL cholesterol and total cholesterol.

There are other benefits associated with green teas some of which are mild and therefore aren't detailed herein. However, one thing is clear, green teas are not only suitable for quenching your thirst but that green cup will help in boosting your health and providing protection against numerous infections.

Chapter 3 – Black Tea (Varieties, Health Benefits, Steeping)

Black tea is popular throughout the world, although it is not very popular in the United States where many people prefer or are more familiar with herbal and green teas. Black tea is grown in different countries but the major producers include China, Kenya, Egypt, and India among others. It should be noted that Black Tea typically has the highest caffeine content as compared to other teas, though not nearly as much as found in coffee. Below are some of the most common types of black teas:

List of Black Teas (9 Varieties)

Yunnan Black tea: - This Chinese black tea is grown in the Yunnan province. It is available in a number of varieties including Yunnan pure gold, Yunnan gold, and broken Yunnan. A high grade Yunnan tea has a sweet aroma and is less bitter compared to other black teas.

Lapsang Souchong: - The preparation of Lapsang Souchong tea is one of the most dramatic. It is withered over cedar or pine fires, pan fried, rolled and then oxidized. Once this is done, it is then put in bamboo baskets for drying over burning pine. This black tea is a little bit bitter and comes in a distinct smoky fragrance.

Keemun black tea: - This tea has a fruity and winey taste with a fruity aroma. It also has a hint of dried plum, pine, and floweriness in its aroma thus giving is a unique and balanced taste. Keemun black tea is a little bit bitter compared to other black teas with a more defined smokiness depending with the processing and variety. Generally, this black tea has a number of varieties including Keemun Gongfu or Congou, Keemun Xin Ya, Hubei Keemun, Keemun Hao Ya and Keemun Mao Feng.

Jiaqu Wuling: - This Chinese tea is also known as black dragon and many people mistake it for Oolong tea. Jiaqu Wuling is fully fermented and comes in a coppery color and is appreciated for its unique relaxing taste.

Tibeti black tea: - Grown in Sichuan Province, Tibeti tea has been around for centuries. It also goes by the name brick tea and has a unique taste.

Darjeeling: - Otherwise known as Champagne of black teas, Darjeeling is produced in India. It is very popular among black tea lovers and comes in a number of varieties depending on its fineness and harvesting period. The champagne of black teas is grown at an elevation of 6000ft and above around the foothills of the Himalayas. The finest of the picks is harvested around March while the second pick is done in May and June. Overall, the tea is highly prized and appreciated for its musky, tannic, and sweet taste.

Nilgiri: - This black tea is also produced in India within Nilgiri which is the second biggest tea growing region in the country. This black tea is grown in elevations of between 1000 and 6000 feet and it has a strong flavor and aroma. To dilute its strong flavor (albeit sweet, smooth, and fruity), this black tea is normally mixed together with other weaker black teas.

Assam: - Assam black tea comes in a number of harvesting cycles and it is the most grown and most popular tea in India. The first Assam tea harvest is done for 10 weeks starting from March while the second is normally scheduled to begin from June. The production takes place through the summer season and early weeks of fall. Its flavor is said to be brisk and malty.

Ceylon black teas: - These black teas are also known as Ceylon tea and are grown in Sri Lanka. They come in different varieties which are classified based on their growing elevations. Generally, Ceylon teas have a light taste with a crisp flavor. Some of the most famous varieties include Nuwara, Uva, Dambulla, Morawak, Eliya, Dickoya, Kandy and Korale.

Generally, black tea is graded on 4 different scales of quality. The highest quality is produced from whole tea leafs while the second rated black tea is normally produced from broken leafs. The other grades are fannings and dusts which lack the typical sweetness associated with black teas, have a darker color, and don't offer as strong a flavor when brewed.

Black Tea Steeping Recommendations

Black tea is best when steeped with 200 degree F (93 °C) water, or even in boiling water for a stronger cup. It's best steeped between 2-3 minutes before separating the tea from the leaves. Drink when the temperature becomes comfortable for you.

Health Benefits of Black Tea

Without additives and sweeteners, plain black teas have insignificant protein, calories, fat and sodium. And just like all other teas produced from the camellia tea plant, black teas are rich in polyphenols which act as antioxidants. Black teas are also known to lower blood pressure.

Research has also shown that consuming black teas on long and short-term basis can help people with coronary artery disease by reversing endothelial vasomotor dysfunction. Black tea also has an aflavin derivative known as Theaflavin-3-gallate which helps to reduce the absorption of cholesterol into the mixed micelle system. Black tea also has a high level of caffeine and therefore can help in boosting energy. Additionally, drinking black tea can help in preventing diseases such as cancer, stroke, and heart disease and also assist in lowering cholesterol due to the presence of thearubinins and theaflavins. Studies have also shown that black tea may help to protect the lungs from damage caused by exposure to cigarette smoke, so if you're a smoker, consider adding black tea to your daily routine.

CHAI TEA (made with black tea)

Chai is another popular kind of tea in many cultures of the world. It is normally prepared by combining different ingredients such as rich black tea, milk, and sometimes spices based on the drinker's preference. Some people opt for sweeteners while others do not. Some of the common spices used in chai include tea masala and ginger.

Health Benefits of Chai

Chai is generally considered helpful for promoting digestion largely because of the additives, and fighting free radicals and improving general health for the same reasons listed above relating to black tea.

Chai preparation

To prepare chai, you will need to place equal measures of water and milk in a tea pot and allow it to low boil. Add 2 teaspoons of tea leaves and whisk occasionally. Allow it a steeping time of 5 to 10 minutes. Then sieve to separate the leaves from the tea, and serve hot or warm.

Chapter 4 – White Tea (Varieties, Health Benefits, Steeping)

As with the other types of teas, white tea is produced from the camellia tea plant. It is specifically made from the youngest tea leaves and tea buds, and is very rare since it is the least processed of all teas. Once the young leaves and buds are harvested, they are steamed before being dried. People who have a problem with caffeine will find white tea to be attractive since it has a lower concentration. The tea has a light flavor and color. It is much appreciated due to its natural delicacy and sweetness, its complexity and subtlety. There is very little caffeine in white tea. Below are some of the most common types of white teas:

List of White Teas (10 Varieties)

Silver needle tea: - This Chinese white tea is normally considered to be a "premium" white and is picked only on two specific days of the year. The tea leaves are picked by hand, and since this tea is rare, its pricing is always high. Silver tea is not only used as a beverage but for other purposes such as bathing for skin rejuvenation. The tea has a unique taste that's said to be mild, sweet, silky, and luxurious.

White peony: - This tea is grown in Fujian province of China and just like silver needle tea; it is rare and very expensive.

However, you will find it an amazing choice if you have a taste for white teas. It is sweet, floral, mellow, and fruity. It is normally harvested during the spring season by picking the tinyest buds and leaves only.

Snow Geisha tea: - This white tea is flavored and is made from splendid cherry pieces and the finest tea buds. It offers a wonderful scent and appearance and will give you the best treat at any given time of the day.

White pu-erh tea: - This Chinese white tea is the rarest of all and somehow the oddest of all the white teas. Unlike many other white teas, this variety is grown in high mountainous elevations. The processing method is very labor intensive. This makes the tea costly and rare. One of the most unique things about white pu-erh tea is that is has a slightly sweet taste with almost no bitterness.

Shou Mei white tea: - This is one of the lowest qualities of white tea from China. It has a strong flavor compared to other white teas from the same country.

White Darjeeling: - This white tea is delicate and one of the highest quality from India. It has a beautiful cold color once brewed with a slightly sweet taste. White Darjeeling white tea also has a delicate scent and is one of the finest white teas on the market.

Assam white tea: - This white tea is named after the region where it is grown in India. Although the region is famed for black tea, Assam white tea is of high quality but also very rare. It has a sweet flavor and an exciting scent.

Ceylon white tea: - Ceylon is one of the finest white teas from Sri Lanka. It is a little bit pricy but offers a taste of pine and honey, a unique taste that will excite white tea lovers. Ceylon has a coppery infusion.

Rhino Matcha white tea: - This white tea grown in the highlands of Rift Valley in Kenya provides a blast of energy and is full of rich antioxidants. Its flavor is known to be grassy and floral. It is most often sold as a powder.

Elephant Ivory White Matcha Tea Powder: - This tea is also grown in Kenya, in the highlands of Rift valley, and is made from the youngest leaves of the plant, then grown down into a fine powder. It's known for tasting deep and grassy.

White Tea Steeping Recommendations

White tea is best when steeped with 175 degree F (80 °C) water. Add your favorite loose leave white tea and steep for only about 30 seconds, or follow the specific instructions provided with the tea purchase for best results. Separate the tea from the leaves, and then drink when the temperature becomes comfortable for you.

Health Benefits of White Tea

Of all the different types of teas on the market, white tea is the least oxidized. This means that it is very low in caffeine thus endearing it to many people who want to avoid caffeine. It is uncured and unfermented, and one study showed it has the most potent anti-cancer properties as compared to more processed teas. It also contains catechins which are beneficial for fighting free radicals. Other health benefits attributed to white tea include:

- It helps in treatment of diabetes

- Prevents risks of cancer, heart disease and stroke.

- Boosts healthy bones, teeth and gums owing to its high levels of fluoride and calcium.

Chapter 5 – Oolong Tea (Varieties, Health Benefits, Steeping)

Oolong is a Chinese name which roughly translates to black dragon. Oolong tea is made from the leaves of Camellia tea plant which are processed over wood or charcoal giving them a rolled or curled shape resembling small black dragons. The processing also gives the tea a unique taste. It is a highly liked tea owing to its health benefits. The tea contains caffeine but at a higher concentration than green tea and a lower concentration than black, and offers a unique taste which is very different from black and green teas. Since it is semi-fermented, Oolong tea doesn't have the same nutritional value of green and white teas. It has an oxidation of between 10% and 70%. Unlike black teas, Oolong teas are prepared immediately after the leaves are harvested by basket-tossing them so as to breakdown the cells found on the leaves' surface. They are then wok fired to stop oxidization. Below are some of the most common types of oolong teas:

List of Oolong Teas (7 Varieties)

Pouchong: - This tea is highly fermented and is processed from long black leaves. It is processed from China and Taiwan and it is one of the most floral of all the Oolong teas. It is very light.

Ti Kuan Yin: - This Oolong tea is tightly pelleted. It is very popular and commonly known as "iron goddess". Ti Kuan Yin is characterized by stout and crinkly leaves. It has a unique apricot, sweet orchid, yet nutty taste.

Formosa: - Formosa Oolong tea is grown in Taiwan. It offers a delicate ripe-fruit taste. It is normally picked in spring season.

Tung Ting: - This Oolong tea is considered to be the finest tea from Taiwan. It is lightly fermented and has a light, gentle, sweet floral taste.

Darjeeling: - This Oolong tea is processed in India. It is a rare first-flush tea with a unique tangy dried fruit taste.

Oriental beauty: - Otherwise known as Dongfang Meiren, this Taiwanese Oolong tea is tippy and comes with natural fruity scent and a sweet taste. Its leaves normally have golden or white tips and once brewed, it has a bright red appearance.

Alishan oolong: - This tea is grown in the Alishan region of Taiwan at an elevation of between 1000 and 1400 ft. It has large rolled leaves and since it is not exposed to much sunlight, the results are a less astringent and sweet fruity flavor. Its leaves have a purple-green color once dried.

Oolong Tea Steeping Recommendations

To get the best results from Oolong teas, the water temperature should be at around 185°-200° F, and steep for 3 to 5 minute. It is however important to read steeping instructions from your tea packet since the temperatures may vary from one tea to the other. You can re-steep Oolong tea multiple times, and you will find the flavor to be a little different (sometimes improved) with each cup.

Health Benefits of Oolong Tea

- Oolong teas have enough caffeine to boost energy in the body

- Since it has some antioxidants, Oolong tea helps prevent different kinds of cancer. The antioxidants help reduce free radicals' damage on body cells and DNA. It should be steeped in very hot water to extract the antioxidants for maximum benefits.

- Oolong tea promotes skin health as the antioxidants present are helpful in toxin removal. By eliminating the toxins, the tea helps prevent skin discoloration and blemishes.

- Promotes weight loss due to the presence of polyphenols. The tea boosts metabolism and this in return helps in weight loss process. Used alongside other activities, the tea can help get good results in fat burning.

- It is also helpful in reducing the risk of cardiovascular diseases as it helps lower cholesterol levels and blood pressure.

Chapter 6 – Rooibos Tea (Varieties, Health Benefits, Steeping)

Rooibos teas are made from Red Bush trees which are commonly found in South Africa. The teas are generally sweet and the processing involves harvesting the leaves from the red bushes before they are grinded and bruised. Once the grinding and bruising processes are complete, the tea is left to ferment and then is dried to generate a reddish brown needle-like tea. Green rooibos tea on the other hand is not fermented and therefore it has a lighter flavor when compared to the red rooibos. Neither green nor red rooibos have any caffeine. Rooibos teas are often mixed with Herbal Teas for improved flavor.

Rooibos Tea Steeping Recommendations

Preparation of rooibos tea doesn't differ much with that of herbal teas. You should bring the water to boil, add your tea into the water, and allow to steep for 5-6 minutes before separating the tea from the leaves. Drink when the temperature is comfortable for you.

Health Benefits of Rooibos Tea

Rooibos tea has high levels of antioxidants including nothofagin and aspalathin. It is also caffeine-free plus it is low in tannin compared to un-oxidized green teas and oxidized black teas. It has numerous phenolic compounds such as flavones, flavanols, dihydrochalcones and flavanones. Also:

- It aids in dealing with digestive problems and helps with nervous tension thus boosting relaxation levels.

- It also helps in fighting different types of cancers

- It is good in alleviating colic, infantile, asthma and dermatological issues.

- It is ideal for people with insomnia as it helps to relax the mind for peaceful sleep.

Chapter 7 – Herbal Tea (Varieties, Health Benefits, Steeping)

Herbal teas have been used for centuries especially due to their health benefits. They are considered medicinal and are made from decoction or infusion of herbs, spices, or different plant materials in hot water. Herbal teas are caffeine-free and are growing in popularity among people who are concerned about their health. There are many herbal teas on the market today but some are more popular than others. Herbal teas contain no caffeine. Below is a list of the major herbal tea varieties and their health benefits.

Peppermint tea: - Has a menthol flavor and its health benefits include treating indigestion, bloating, heartburn, intestinal gas, colds and colic among others.

Sage tea: - It is used to relieve sore throat caused by laryngitis or tonsillitis. It is also used to assist in digestion and relieve constipation.

Chamomile Tea: - Boosts the relaxation of the mind and can help if you want to enjoy a peaceful night's sleep.

Ginger tea: - Processed from ginger roots, it helps deal with symptoms of upset stomach, nausea and sore throat. It can also help in case of colon disorders, menstrual pains, rheumatic and gastrointestinal disorders. Ginger tea also helps to calm motion sickness.

Lemon balm tea: - This tea is a mild antibacterial, sedative and antiviral. It is suitably used to help deal with insomnia, flu, digestive disorders, cold sores, nervous agitation, nausea, indigestion, menstrual cramps and gas among other conditions.

Rosemary tea: - This tea contains antiseptic properties which are ideal for relieving headaches. It is a good stimulant, anti-inflammatory, astringent and diuretic. It stimulates bile flow, circulation and acts as a nervous system balancer. Rosemary tea can also help boost energy levels, regulate blood pressure and acts as an antidepressant.

Hibiscus tea: - Hibiscus is a good source of Vitamin C and works almost the same way as red wine to help the functionality and vitality of the heart. It is rich in antioxidants and thus can help reduce risks or heart diseases and control the level of cholesterol in the body.

Blueberry tea: - This herbal tea is suitable as it revitalizes healing properties. It promotes the functioning of urinary tract and kidneys. It is a good energy booster.

Raspberry Tea: - This herbal tea is helpful in eliminating harmful toxins from the body.

Red clover: - This tea is popular as it helps relieve stomach upsets and soothe in case of common colds.

Rose hips: - Generally used as a source of bioflavonoid and vitamin C which are suitable in boosting kidney, liver and blood tonic. It is also a good remedy for coughs, colds and fatigue.

Parsley tea: - This herbal tea is a diuretic and aids in the functioning of the kidney.

Anise seed: - This tea is helpful in soothing coughs, promotes healthy digestion, improves bronchitis and helps to freshen breathe.

Chrysanthemum tea: - This sweet flavored tea helps to neutralize toxins, protect against possible kidney damage and reduce heat from the body arising from fevers.

Lemon grass tea: - Has amazing relaxing effects. A cup of hot lemon grass will help deal with fatigue and cases of indigestion.

These are just a few of the most popular varieties of herbal teas. There are literally dozens of herbal teas on the market today and each of these offers a host of nutritional properties and health benefits.

Herbal Tea Steeping Recommendations

To prepare herbal teas, you will need to boil the water, add your herbal tea, and allow to steep for 4 to 5 minutes before separating. Stir well and add honey if you wish. Drink only when the water temperature is comfortable.

Conclusion

Tea is the oldest beverage and the health benefits have been established through years of research and numerous scientific studies. It is clear that drinking a few cups of tea every day will help you to enjoy a host of health benefits as your body absorbs various nutrients available from all the different types of teas available.

White it is true that you can benefit greatly from your cup of tea, the process of brewing and steeping time will determine whether you are able to enjoy the best nutrients that are concealed in the tea leaves. It is therefore important to understand how to brew and steep your tea so as to enjoy the nutritional value provided by the tea. Learn which teas can be re-steeped and those that should not to avoid the mistake of messing up the flavor and destroying the minerals found in different tea varieties. Typically, the place of purchase or the packaging on your tea will include all this information.

In addition, the choice of herbal teas should be executed carefully if you are to enjoy the health benefits available for each variety. There is a major difference between herbal teas and those made from the Camellia tea plant. However, there is no denying that both these types of tea are suitable not only for quenching your thirst but also for improving your health. Most herbs from which herbal plants are extracted have been used for years in making herbal medications and there is no doubting that the same effects found in herbal medication can be enjoyed by drinking herbal teas.

When buying herbal teas, it is important to consider buying trusted brands and storing them properly to maintain their health nutrients. Additionally, always remember that the flavor and taste of different tea varieties will be affected by the area where it is grown, the way it is processed, and the harvesting procedure and timing. Different teas can be flavored using various flavors based on the drinker's preference. Consider mixing a tea from the camellia plant with a fruity or flowery herbal tea. No matter what concoction you come up with, it is clear that tea is a healthy drink that's very much worth your purchase and efforts in making it.

Thank you for purchasing this tea guide, and I certainly hope you found it both interesting and useful. If you did, please leave a review on Amazon – I'd greatly appreciate it!

Made in the USA
Monee, IL
02 March 2024

54346255R10036